Food Trucks

Julie Murray

Abdo Kids Junior
is an Imprint of Abdo Kids
abdobooks.com

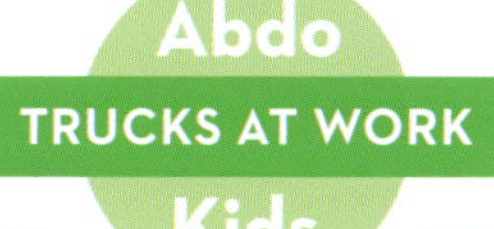

abdobooks.com

Published by Abdo Kids, a division of ABDO, P.O. Box 398166, Minneapolis, Minnesota 55439.

Abdo Kids Junior™ is a trademark and logo of Abdo Kids.

Printed in the United States of America, North Mankato, Minnesota.

052023

092023

THIS BOOK CONTAINS RECYCLED MATERIALS

Photo Credits: Getty Images, Shutterstock

Production Contributors: Teddy Borth, Jennie Forsberg, Grace Hansen

Design Contributors: Candice Keimig, Pakou Moua

Library of Congress Control Number: 2022946715

Publisher's Cataloging-in-Publication Data

Names: Murray, Julie, author.

Title: Food trucks / by Julie Murray

Description: Minneapolis, Minnesota : Abdo Kids, 2024 | Series: Trucks at work | Includes online resources and index.

Identifiers: ISBN 9781098266141 (lib. bdg.) | ISBN 9781098266844 (ebook) | ISBN 9781098267193 (Read-to-me ebook)

Subjects: LCSH: Trucks--Juvenile literature. | Vehicles--Juvenile literature. | Food trucks--Juvenile literature.

Classification: DDC 388.32--dc23

Table of Contents

Food Trucks

Food trucks **prepare**, cook, and sell food.

Surfside
SEAFOOD &
LOBSTER ROLL
Lobster/Shrimp/Crab on "Texas"
Garlic-toasted New England Roll... $10
Capt. Kyle's
DELICIOUS
Combo
$3
Point Break
PO-BOYS
Fried Clam
OR Fried Shrimp
Good Tastes, Tastes Good
we deliver
TIP

They are restaurants on wheels!

678.231.5151
www.ANGELFIRE7BBQ.com
ANGELFIRE 7 BBQ
freckled & blue
freckledandblue.com
Southern Eatery
Arts

The taco truck is here.

Marco gets extra salsa.

MOTOWN
TACOS
OPEN

The **BBQ** truck is here.

Ribs are on the menu!

The pizza truck is here. It has a lot of good toppings.

Vegetarian
Curry Chicken
Seafood
BBQ Chicken
CRISPY PIZZA
CRISPY PIZZA
Tom Yam Kung
Carbonara
CRISPY PIZZA
ISPY PIZZA
Crispy Pizza
CRISPY PIZZA

The burger truck is here.

Lon orders veggie burgers.

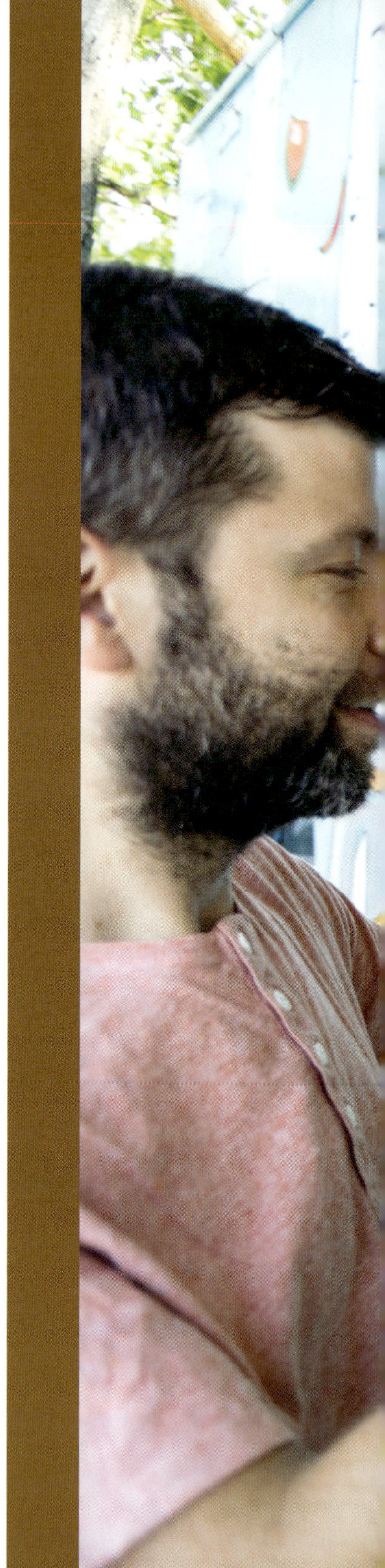

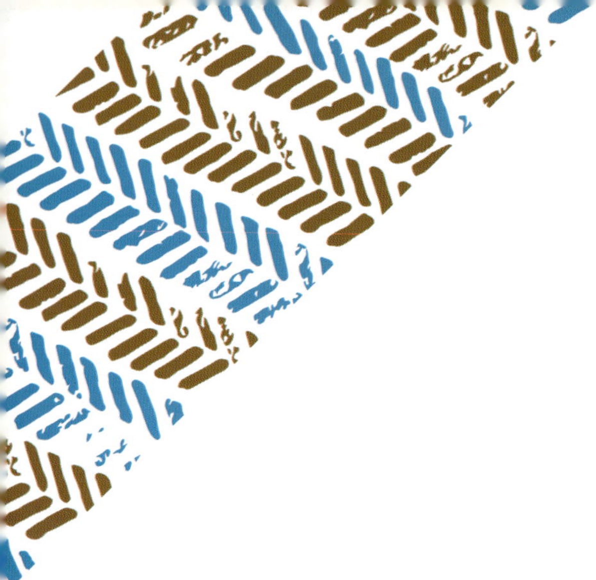

The donut truck is here.

The donuts are colorful!

TOBLERONE
nutella
DONUTS
Jean Paul
TONIO'S
hvetemel-soyamel-sukker-vegetabilsk olje raps
skummel kuspulver-bake pulver-egg plommer pulver

The ice cream truck is here.

It has fun flavors!

59 St - Columbus Cir
A C B D 1
SUNDAES · SHAKES
FUN-TIME
SMOOTHIE INC.
328 TEN-EYCK ST.
BK. N.Y. 11206
FUN-TIME MILKSHAKE

Have you eaten at a food truck?

Lomito Gourmet
Peruvian Cuisine
LOMO SALTADO
CEVICHE MIXTO
SALCHI PAPAS
LomitoGourmet.com
Lomito Gourmet Denver
Coca-Cola

More Food Trucks

dessert truck

hot dog truck

pasta truck

sandwich truck

Glossary

BBQ
short for barbecue.

prepare
to make ready.

Index

Visit **abdokids.com** to access crafts, games, videos, and more!

Use Abdo Kids code

TFK6141

or scan this QR code!

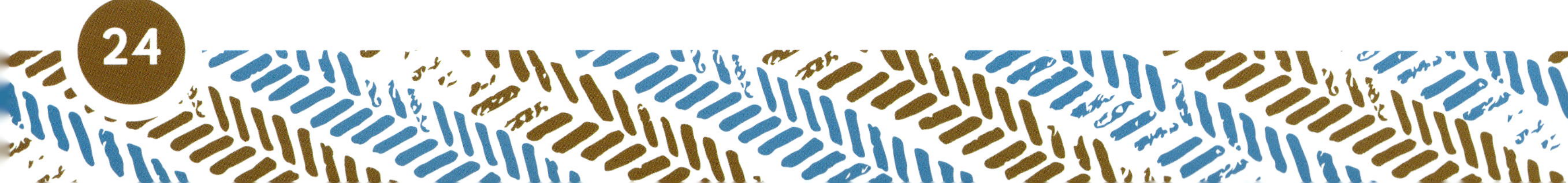